T0022660

LETTERS FROM MONTREAL